From Afte to Yellow Boots

A Glossary of Seamus Heaney's
Hearth Language

MAURA JOHNSTON

Colmcille
Press

Published December 2020, reprinted November 2021 by
COLMCILLE PRESS
Ráth Mór Centre
Bligh's Lane
Derry BT48 0LZ
www.colmcillepress.com

Colmcille Press gratefully acknowledges the support of the Forge Writers Group with this
publication.

Edited by Garbhán Downey/Forge Writers Group
Layout/design by Joe McAllister, Hive Studios – www.hivestudio.org

A CIP catalogue record for this book is available from the British Library.

ISBN 978 1 914009 01 3

To Deirdre, who shared a love of words

ABOUT THE AUTHOR

Maura Johnston is a writer and educator. Her writings include the poetry collections Just Suppose and The Whetstone. She has lived for most of her life in South Derry.

Over the past fifteen years she has worked in schools and with community groups exploring the works and language of Seamus Heaney.

CONTENTS

ACKNOWLEDGEMENTS

I am grateful to Garbhán Downey who believed in this project. Thank you to the family of Seamus Heaney for their support. Jane McNally helped source many of the artefacts photographed, and corroborated the use of dialect words.

Thanks to the many family members and friends who use this dialect and were willing to share their knowledge of it. Thank you to Joe McAllister for providing photographs which admirably support the text. Kevin Johnston also provided photographs and drew the maps.

Heartfelt thanks to Colmcille Press for their excellent production of the book, to Martina Gorman, for her meticulous arrangement of the index, and to Joe Martin of the Forge Writers Group for his invaluable input.

INTRODUCTION

> The point about dialect or hearth language is its complete propriety to the speaker and his or her voice and place. What justifies it and gives it original juice and joy is intimacy and inevitability. I've always confined myself to words I myself could have heard spoken, words I'd be able to use with familiarity in certain companies.
>
> *Stepping Stones: Interviews with Seamus Heaney*, page 129

Language, the medium used by a writer, is a living thing; it changes over time. Each year words in common usage are added to dictionaries. With the rapid progress in science and technology in the past twenty years, many of these additions have their origin in these subjects. Of course sometimes is merely an added layer of meaning to an already existing word, such as the word *mouse*.

Currently, words are lost to language. Words die from lack of use. Words thrive when they are part of everyday vocabulary, spoken and written.

In many of his writings Seamus Heaney uses *hearth language* or dialect. His phrase *hearth language* is apposite. It is the language we learn and use at first within the family and then, as our horizons widen, within the local community. In these places we are secure, at home and understood.

We are using dialect, regional linguistic variation, variations of pronunciation, vocabulary or grammar of the language used by a particular group in a community or country. Dialect gives a sense of rootedness, of access to a specific culture, a notion of belonging, a stand against the idea of a state having a monolingual identity.

Since it is common to one particular community or class there may be a feeling of social and cultural inclusion for those speaking a particular dialect and, conversely, of exclusion in those who are not familiar with it. So, to fully engage with a piece of writing it is better not to feel excluded, by gaining some idea of what dialect words might mean.

This glossary concerns itself with a small area of the north of Ireland, a region where people speak English, an English enriched by dialect words having their roots in Irish and Scots Gaelic, Lowland Scots, Anglo Saxon and Elizabethan English. For centuries these words were in common use, but I have found that this aspect of language is changing.

I am almost of an age, come from the same region and have the same background as Seamus Heaney. The words he uses are familiar to me, were used in my childhood home and the community in which I grew.

But in my work as facilitator for reminiscence groups, and in schools and adult groups for creative writing I have come to the realisation that understanding of our local dialect has diminished, and in some cases, disappeared.

This is due to many things. Globalisation promotes levelling of language. This is reinforced by access to technologies – television, social media, computers – which use language with a vocabulary created to be understood by people wherever they might live. It is also a result of decisions made about what vocabulary we need to function in the modern world.

The Lost Words, by Robert MacFarlane, is a book which responds to the withdrawal from dictionaries of words concerning the natural world. In his introduction Robert MacFarlane says, "Once upon a time words began to vanish from the language of children. They disappeared so quietly that at first almost no one noticed – fading away like water on stone."

I feel that is exactly is what is happening with our local dialect, the vocabulary used by Seamus Heaney. While reading his poetry with groups of local children and young adults, it is clear that these words are no longer hearth language. And if people from Seamus Heaney's own home place are having difficulty understanding some of his words, how much more difficult it must be for those for whom English is not a first language or who do not share his cultural and linguistic background.

While elucidation and, it is hoped to at least some extent, preservation of dialect was the initial impetus for this glossary, other considerations were taken into account. Society, farming, expectations have changed a great deal in the generations that have passed since Seamus Heaney first published his work. So some of the customs he mentions, ways of family life and of working, have been given longer explanation to clarify them.

This glossary has been written in the hope that it will help readers of Seamus Heaney's poetry and plays, that the explanations will enrich their reading and that it helps preserve his hearth language.

Maura Johnston, 2020

SEAMUS HEANEY'S BELLAGHY

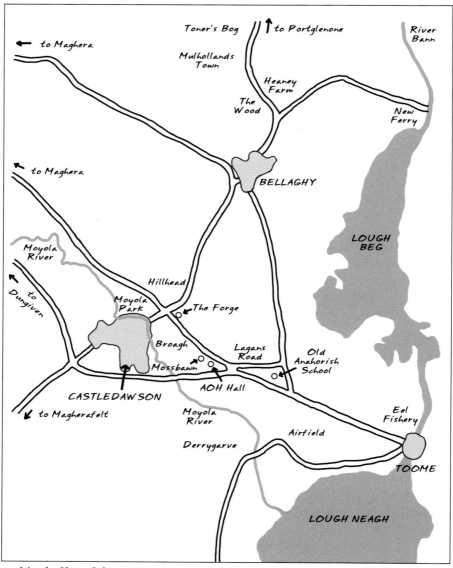

Map by Kevin Johnston.

BELLAGHY TOWNLANDS

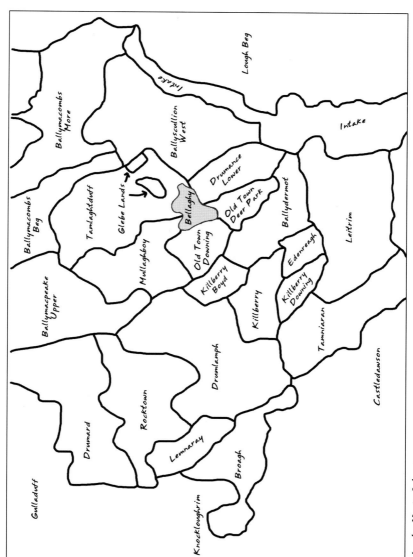

Map by Kevin Johnston.

PART ONE

Glossary of Hearth Terms

...A...

afterbirth
The afterbirth (the placenta and membranes expelled after a calf's birth) was also called the cleaning. It used to be spread on a hedge, preferably a thorn hedge. There are various theories for this custom. Some say it guaranteed good health for the calf, others say it was to stop dogs from eating it.

aftergrass
Grass which grows after hay has been cut, or grass which grows amongst the stubble after the harvest.

a hard station
A difficult situation; a hard time.

allow
Admit; suppose.

althing
Parliament; assembly; gathering.

All Saints
The day after Hallowe'en, a feast day when the Catholic Church celebrates the lives of saints and martyrs, and remembers in a special way all the souls in heaven. At this time of year the veil between this life and the next is said to be thin, and it is thought by some the dead can slip back to visit familiar places.

All Souls
Religious feast celebrated on November 2. On this day, prayers are offered for the souls of those who have died but not yet entered heaven.

antic
Light hearted; amusing; lively.

anvil
A heavy iron block used by a blacksmith to hammer and shape metal.

apron
A protective garment often worn by women, which covers the front of the clothes and is tied at the back.

apron bib
The top portion of the apron which slips over the neck.

ashpan
A metal tray which collects ashes and cinders under a fire grate.

ash-pit
The area under a fire or barbeque where ashes are collected.

ash-plant
A stick or staff made of an ash sapling, which was favoured by cattle drovers.

astray
Having lost one's wits; away from the right path. There was a belief that in some fields the fairies would send a mist that would lead a person astray and they wouldn't be able to find their way out of it.

away in the head
See: Is his head away?

awn
A stiff bristle, especially one of those growing from the ear or flower of barley, **rye**, or some other grasses.

aye
Yes.

...B...

bad cess
Bad luck; misfortune.

bag-apron
An apron usually worn when doing farm work outside the house. It consisted of a hessian sack, probably one which had held potatoes or meal. This sack was wound around the waist and fastened at the back – sometimes with a six-inch nail.

bakeboard
A wooden board on which bread was kneaded and pastry rolled.

baler
A tractor-drawn machine which goes around and around the rows in a hayfield, picking up the hay, pressing it into compact bales, and then expelling them. Bales are sometimes rectangular and come out bound with twine. Modern bales are often cylindrical in shape and wrapped in plastic sheeting.

bane
A cause of harm; continuous annoyance.

banshee
From the Irish 'bean sídhe', woman of the fairy mound (woman fairy). The cry of the banshee presages a death in the family. The death might even be of someone living abroad. Some believe that the banshee usually foretells the death of a member of families whose surname began with 'O' 'Mac' or 'Mc', such as O'Brien or McGarvey.

barrow (stone-roofed barrow)
A barrow is a mound of earth
which covers a prehistoric tomb.

bath
Before the 1950s few houses in
rural Ireland had water piped
into their houses. A bath then
would not have been plumbed in
in a permanent position. It would
have been made of galvanized
iron and stored in an outhouse.
On bath night it was brought
into the kitchen to be near the
supply of hot water which would
have been boiling on the stove or
hearth fire.

bawn
From 'babhún', the Irish for
cattle enclosure, a bawn is the
part of a castle or farmhouse
grounds which is enclosed or
fortified, and normally used to
keep cattle safe.

beating flax
Before the invention of the
scutcher, women beat flax with
sticks to remove woody fibres.

bed the stall
When cows were kept in the byre
over the winter the floor was
cleaned and swept every day. The
dung and old straw was put on
the duchall (dunghill/midden)
and then clean straw for bedding
was put on the floor of each stall.

beestings
Milk from the first few milkings
of a cow which has calved. It is
very rich and provided immunity
to the calf. It was often cooked to
a thick custard and considered a
delicacy for family.

beetled
Beetling; pounding. Flax stalks
can be beetled. Linen cloth is
pounded to tighten the weave and
give it a sheen.

beets
A sheaf of flax, usually tied with a
band of grass or rushes.

bell
(v) To make a ringing sound like
a bell; to bellow like the noise of
rutting deer.

bellyband
Part of a horse's harness – a loose
strap passing outside the girth.

benweed
Ragwort; a yellow flowering plant
which is toxic to cattle if they eat
too much of it.

besom
(n) A besom is a brush or broom
consisting of twigs tied around a
stick.

besoming
Brushing (with a besom).

beyond the pale
Outside accepted behavior; beyond limits. The phrase originated in the fourteenth century when the safe or acceptable place to be in Ireland, in the minds of the English occupiers, was within the Pale, the area around Dublin, which fell under their authority. Pale here refers to paling or a fenced area i.e. a boundary.

bia
From the Irish 'bia', food.

billhook
A tool used in agriculture for cutting shrubs or small woody material. It has a wooden handle and crescent shaped blade with a sharp inner edge.

birl/burl
Turn; spin; whirl; toss; argument; noise of an argument.

bitted
Having the bit fitted into a horse's mouth. The bit, made of metal or synthetic material, is a part of the harness. It is attached to the bridle and helps the rider to guide the horse.

blackout blinds
Blinds or window coverings, made of a thick or dark material which does not allow light to penetrate. Their use was mandatory during the blackout of the Second World War.

blackthorn
A stick made of wood from the blackthorn tree. The stick can have a polished or natural finish. Traditionally the blackthorn stick was used not only as a walking stick but as a weapon. The knob, which is part of the root, was solid and capable of causing damage. Nowadays the blackthorn is normally used only as a walking stick. The blackthorn tree is associated with the fairies and it is supposed to be unlucky to cut one down.

blather/blether
(v) To talk a lot; talk nonsense.
(n) A person who talks a lot or talks nonsense.

bleaching-green
A grassy area where linen was spread out to whiten in the sunshine.

bleb
Blister; bulge; bubble; bubble of air.

blet/bletted/blettings
Overripe; almost rotten; decomposing.

bleyberries
Bilberries.

blight, blighted root, blighted
Blight is a disease which affects potatoes. Blight first affects the leaves, then travels down the stem to the tubers, which rot. In Ireland in the 19th century the most common species of potato grown was the lumper. Whole crops of these potatoes were destroyed by blight several times, leading to periods of great hunger or famine.

blinked
It was believed some people could blink, or put the blink on, someone or something. This was a curse, an attempt to bring bad luck. If someone put the blink on your hens they would stop laying. Or if your milk was blinked, the butter would not come when you churned. (See also: churn.)

blinkers/winkers
Part of a horse's harness. Blinkers are attached to the bridle. They are cup shaped and used to stop the horse seeing what is behind or to the side. They help the horse to look straight ahead without distraction.

blood pudding
A sausage generally made with pork fat, pork blood and oatmeal, also called black pudding. Often included in food fried for breakfast.

bluestone
There is no known cure for potato blight, although measures can be taken to prevent it. Bluestone can be used as a preventative. Bluestone (copper sulphate) is added to a mixture of washing soda and hot water. On a dry day this is sprayed on the potato plants, ensuring the undersides of the leaves are covered, as well as the tops.

bog
An area of wet ground made up of dead plant material which has turned into peat. The peat, or turf, can be cut and dried and used as fuel.

bogbanks
An area in a turf bog where turf/peat is cut for fuel.

bog-berry
Normally means a small cranberry, but could be blueberry/blaeberry/bilberry in Ireland.

bog-cotton
A plant which thrives in bogland. The two most common in Ireland are, Common Cotton Grass and Hare's Tail. Both produce white, fluffy flowers.

bogging in
Starting energetically; getting stuck in; tucking into food.

bolster
A long pillow, suitable for a double bed.

boltered
Hair matted with blood.

bone-lappings
The ligaments of a person or animal, which connect a bone/joint to muscle.

book
See: the book.

boons
Blessings; benefits; advantages; help; bonuses.

boortree
An elder tree.

bore the brunt
Suffered the worst effects.

boreen
A small road.

Bothy (pl. bothies)
A small hut; shed; outside lavatory.

bottoms
Flat and wet marshy land.

bourne, shadow-bourne
Goal; destination; boundary.

bow-saw
A saw with a narrow, detachable blade attached to a handle and bent like an archer's bow.

boyo
Man, lad, rascal.

brae
Small slope or hill.

braird
New growth; shoots of grass or grain crops.

briars
Thorny shrubs or bushes like those which produce wild roses or blackberries.

Brigid's Cross
Brigid's crosses are made on the feast of the saint, February 1. With St Patrick and St Colmcille, St Brigid is one of the patron saints of Ireland. Her cross is made of rushes and has four arms. The crosses are hung in dwelling houses and byres to bring protection from evil and disease.

bullaun
From the Irish 'bullán', a bullaun is the term for a depression or hollow in a stone in which

rainwater may collect. Some people believe this water has healing properties.

burled
Whirled; hurried.

burn
A small river; a stream.

buttermilk
The liquid left after milk-churning, when the butter has been removed. It can be used for baking. Traditionally buttermilk was drunk with dinner.

butter-print
A wooden mould, often with a design carved into it, which was used to shape butter.

butter-spades
Wooden spades, usually ridged, used to form butter into pounds, half pounds or little balls.

buttery
A storeroom for food and wine.

byre
The building cows came into for milking. Each cow had its own stall, and was chained while being milked. The milker sat on a milking stool, a three legged stool, and milked into a tin can. As this can filled, the milk was poured into a bucket.

...C...

cailleach
In Celtic mythology, the cailleach was the goddess of the harvest. The term, which comes from the old Irish word 'caillech', meaning 'veiled one', was later used to refer to an old woman (usually wise), a witch, an old hag or crone, or a nun.

cairn
A man-made mound of stones; stones piled up as a memorial or landmark.

cairnstone
The stones which are used to build a cairn.

camlet
Strong waterproof cloth; originally a fabric made from camel hair or angora wool.

canny, canniness
Shrewd; careful; competent; prudent.

cantreds
Districts, each made up of one hundred villages.

canty
Thorough; tidy; cheerful; neat.

catchpenny
Something on offer or for sale which is attractive and desirable but is, in reality, worthless; something to catch the money of a foolish person.

causey
A pathway across a bog or wet place; a paved path; a causeway.

Celtic cross
A Celtic cross is a cross with a nimbus or circle surrounding the intersection of stem and arms. Often the cross is decorated with intertwining Celtic art designs. There are, in many parts of Ireland, Celtic high crosses made of stone. These have, as well as abstract decorations, carved figures showing religious scenes.

chaff
The husks of grain separated by threshing; debris; detritus.

chancy
Good looking; lucky; fortunate. Involving risk.

chow
Chew.

churl
A peasant; a countryman; someone with rough manners; a rude person.

churn
(v) To agitate cream or milk until butter forms.
(n) The container into which the milk to be churned is put. Traditional churns were made of wood, without nails and banded with metal hoops. The wooden lid had a hole in it through which went a wooden plunger, or dasher. This was moved up and down till the butter was formed. It took a long time and was tiring work. If a visitor came while it was going on, it was considered good manners to offer to take a turn at the churning.

clabber, clabbery
Thick, sticky mud. The sort of mud found where cattle have churned up wet ground at, for example, a gap in a hedge. (See also: gap.)

clamping
Building a stack or mound of turf or potatoes.

clout
(n) A slap, usually on the head; a heavy blow.
(v) To hit someone hard; punch; pound; slap.

colloguing
Talking; conferring; talking confidentially; conspiring.

colly
Smuts; specks of coal dust; soot.

Conway Stewart
A brand of fountain pen. A fountain pen was a treasured possession. It was a big advance on the dip pen. When using the latter, the nib had to be dipped in ink, and dipped again after writing just a few words. The barrel of a fountain pen could be unscrewed to reveal an inner rubber tube which held a reservoir of ink. When the nib of the pen was inserted in ink and this tube depressed, the tube filled with ink. One could write longer texts before the pen needed refilling.

coof
A stupid fellow; dolt; lout; fool.

coracle
A boat like a curragh, made of skin or canvas stretched over a wooden frame.

corpse house
Literally a house with a corpse in it; a wake house.

corrugated iron
Sheets of galvanized iron shaped into parallel grooves, often used for roofing.

cow-parsley
Wild chervil; a plant found in hedgerows, having fern like leaves and heads of lacy white flowers.

crab-apple jelly
A red or golden jelly made from crab apples. These apples grow wild. They are very small, bitter apples, too small to peel, so perfect for jelly making. The jelly is usually flavoured with cloves.

craking
Talking incessantly; talking persistently; complaining or whining.

crane
Over an open-hearth fire, the crane was the hook from which pots (or the griddle) were suspended.

crannog
An artificial island, mostly used as a home for extended families, built on lakes or in estuaries.

creek
A narrow river; a tidal inlet off a shoreline; a channel in a marsh.

creel
A wickerwork basket.

crock
An earthenware container with a glazed interior. It was usually

wider at the top than the bottom. It was used to hold drinking water and milk. Several days' milk would be stored in a crock until it was ready for churning.

cribs
The rails around a cart or trailer to help keep in the load.

croppies
Irishmen who rose up against the English forces in 1798. The rebels cropped their hair short, hence the term Croppies.

cross-cut
A type of saw used to cut trees, logs or firewood. It was worked by two people, one on either side of the wood being sawn, pushing and pulling in rhythm. The teeth were designed to cut on the pull stroke in each pulling direction.

cub
A boy.

cudding
Chewing their cud; cud is soft food sent up from the stomach where it went when first swallowed. It is re-chewed and swallowed again, going to a different part of the stomach. Animals with more than one stomach, e.g. cows, can do this.

cures
Folk remedies.

currachs
Currachs are boats. There are various types. One type is wooden framed with animal skin or canvas stretched over it. Others incorporate wickerwork, wood, masts and sails.

cut out the tongue
For a time, a bounty (or sum of money as a reward) would be paid to anyone who could produce a dead fox, or the tongue of a fox, at a police station. Showing the tongue was a strategy designed to prevent the same fox being presented more than once (to claim a second bounty). Sometimes the police would nick the tongue, for the same reason.

...D...

dailigone
Dusk; twilight.

dandered, (dandering)
Strolled; walked slowly or aimlessly.

dandled
Rocked; swayed.

dawdle
Walk slowly; move slowly.

dealing-men
Men who bought and sold, particularly those who bought and sold livestock. Dealing was mainly done at fairs.

deem
Suppose.

diatomite
A fine-grained, sedimentary rock. Diatomite was found along the banks of the River Bann and is known locally as Bann Clay. It was used for insulation and to make bricks.

dinnsheanchas
Literature that deals with placenames.

dishabills
Underwear; nightwear. From the French 'déshabillé', the state of being partly or scantily clothed.

diviner
Someone who can detect a spring or water source by holding the two short ends of a forked hazel stick. The presence of water is indicated when the stick jerks in the hand of the diviner. Some people have the gift of divining.

do your station
Do your share of suffering; literally carry out the penance of a pilgrimage to St Patrick's Purgatory in Lough Derg.

docken
A dock plant, believed to ease the pain of nettle stings when rubbed on the affected part.

dote
(v) To idolise someone; love fondly and uncritically; treasure. (n) One who is doted upon; one held dear.

douce
Sweet, gentle, steady, reliable.

draw-well
A deep well from which water is drawn up with a bucket fastened to a rope or chain, rather than having the water dipped out with a container held in the hand. Sometimes a windlass (a hand-operated winching crane) is used.

dreeps
Drips.

drench
To soak. Farmers would treat sick cattle by putting medicine in a bottle, keeping the animal's mouth open and, from the side, putting the bottle over the back of the tongue as far back as possible, tilting it to pour the liquid gradually down the throat. The

animal's head would be held up to prevent the medicine running out. Often a difficult procedure.

drillie
A drill instructor at school; a physical education teacher.

drouth
Dryness; thirst; drought. A drouth may refer to a person who is fond of alcoholic drinks.

drover
Someone who guides cattle along, drives them in the right direction, by walking behind them and urging them on.

drover's cane
A stick, commonly an ash plant, used by someone driving cattle. It could be used both as a staff to support the drover as he walked or to smack the hindquarters of the cattle to encourage them to move. (See also: ash plant.)

duchall, duchal
A manure heap; dunghill; midden (from Scots). When a byre got its daily cleaning the dung and straw would be wheeled to the duchall and thrown on it. Once a year the manure from the duchall was spread on the fields to fertilise them. When the term duchall is applied to a person it suggests laziness or uselessness.

dun
A fort (from the Irish, dún).

dung
Animal waste; manure.

dunghill
See duchall.

dungy
Dirty; smelly.

dunt
A thump or a blow, often given by the elbow or the head.

dunting
Sound of something bumping into an object.

...E...

Easter water
Easter water is special holy water. It is the water that is blessed during the liturgical ceremonies in Catholic churches on Holy Saturday. It is used in baptisms. The faithful take bottles of Easter water home to sprinkle in rooms and outhouses to bring blessings and grace to the household.

eelskin
Eelskins were supposed to have curative properties. Fresh, moist eelskin would be wrapped around

a sprain and left to dry on the limb. This eelskin bandage would be worn as long as necessary. Oil obtained when eels were slowly fried was stored and used to massage aching joints.

eked
Made farmyard-animal sounds; squeaked.

elder
Local pronunciation of a cow's udder.

empery
Command; absolute control; dominion.

Erenach
An Irish person; someone with ecclesiastical duties.

'ESN'
Educationally 'subnormal' – an outdated classification for pupils needing special or remedial help.

ewe-leaze
Summer pasture for sheep.

· · • F • · ·

fair
A gathering in a town or village for the buying and selling of livestock.

fair day
Each town had a specific day each month for holding the livestock fair.

fair-hill
In a town where a fair was held there was a green space called the fair-hill. Here cattle could be displayed and prospective buyers could move around looking at the animals before deciding which ones to buy. On the fair-hill or on the street, horses could be run to show their paces.

fanked
Penned up (as in sheep); twisted (as in cloth or rope).

fare
Get along, proceed, make out.

fast days
Days designated by the Catholic Church when eating was restricted. Every day in Lent, except Sunday, was a fast day for adults over twenty-one years and under sixty, with the exception of pregnant women or the sick. On a fast day, each adult was allowed one unrestricted main meal and two collations where the food in total could not exceed twelve ounces in weight.

fasting spittle
Saliva produced in the morning before the fast has been broken. This spittle is supposed to be effective in curing some diseases.

fealty
Fidelity; formal, sworn loyalty, to a lord.

felloes
The outer rim of a wheel, to which the spokes are fixed.

Fenians
Members of the Irish Republican Brotherhood, who campaigned during the late nineteenth and early twentieth centuries to free Ireland from British rule. Used more recently in slang as a term for an Irish Catholic or a nationalist/republican.

fine-combing, fine-combed
The use of a fine comb to search the hair thoroughly for the presence of head lice and nits; the act of searching, examining every detail.

firebox
The part of a fireplace or stove where the fuel is burned.

first-footing
A tradition, practised mainly in Scotland, of being the first person to cross the threshold of a house after midnight on New Year's Eve. The first-footer should be dark haired; a red-haired person is unlucky. The first-footer brings symbols of prosperity – a lump of coal, bread, salt and perhaps a measure of whisky.

flabby
Soft; loose.

flail
A tool which was used to beat grain crops to separate the grain from the straw. There are three parts to a flail – the wooden handle, the beater (swipple) usually made of wood, generally hazel, and the moveable joint. The beater was heavier than the handle and was fastened to it with a joint made of flax or sheepskin or goatskin.

flashlamp
A battery-powered torch.

flax
The plant from which linen is made.

flax-dam
A pool or dam of still water, where flax plants are left to rot in order to loosen the fibres. As the flax rots it produces gases with noxious smells.

flour sack

Bread was baked daily in most houses. Flour was bought in 3lb, 6lb or two-stone bags. These bags or sacks were made of fine cotton. Thrifty housewives made use of the empty sacks. They were boiled to clean them and remove the name and logo of the manufacturer. They were made into petticoats, pillowcases, sheets and used as nappies and dishcloths. A very popular provider of flour was Early Riser.

fodder

The hay given to cattle in winter months.

foggage

In winter the grass which has been uncut in the summer and left for the cattle to eat; second growth of grass; the practice of leaving cattle in the fields.

fort

A fort, ráth or hill fort was a defensive structure built to protect people and livestock from marauders. In Ireland, they were usually circular earthen works with ditches around the perimeter. Sometimes there were wooden fences and buildings. They are often marked now by a ring of trees or thorn bushes. Some of them are believed to be the home of the little folk and are called Fairy Forts.

forty days of fast

The season of Lent in Christian churches. This is the period between Ash Wednesday and Holy Saturday (the eve of Easter Sunday). During this time, the churches laid down regulations for fasting. Many people added their own privations – for example, giving up sugar and milk for the duration of Lent.

'Forty-five

The years 1845 to 1852 saw the potato harvest in Ireland blighted. For most Irish people, potatoes were the staple food in their diet, so as a result of the blight and the failure of the potato crop, this period was known as the Great Hunger or the Great Famine. During these years the population of Ireland dropped by twenty-five percent. One million people died of starvation and one million emigrated, mainly to the United States, but some to Canada, Scotland or England.

foster brother/sister

For centuries in Ireland, it was customary to foster out children, boys and girls. This meant handing them over to another family to be reared and taught what they needed to know for their station in life. Some were handed at birth to a wet nurse, some left home around the age of seven. The natural children in the foster family were foster brothers and sisters. Often a strong bond developed, as important as a blood tie.

fosterling
One who was fostered.

fother
Local pronunciation of fodder, the hay given to cattle in the winter months.

foxfire
The bluish green light given off by some species of fungi which grows on decaying wood. It is also known as fairy fire.

furrow
A groove or trench in the ground made by a plough, to prepare a field for planting.

furtherance
Advancement.

Furthering, furthered
Bringing forward; advancing.

...G...

Gaeltacht
An Irish-speaking region. Surviving **Gaeltachts** include areas of counties Donegal, Mayo, Galway and Kerry, and parts of some other Irish counties. In Gaelteacht areas Irish, or Gaelic, is the first language of the residents and is the language of everyday interaction. Students wishing to improve their knowledge of Irish go to summer schools in these areas.

gallivant, gallivanting
To roam around in search of amusement.

gallowglass
Gallowglasses were mercenaries from Scotland. Large numbers of them settled in Ireland where they were welcomed, not least because they were trained, heavily-armoured soldiers.

gap
A space cut in a hedge to allow passage between one field and another, sometimes closed with a gate. This gate was often made of strands of barbed wire, stapled to upright posts.

glar
Thick sticky mud.

glarry
Wet; muddy; oozy.

glib
Historically in Ireland a mass of matted hair worn over the eyes.

glit
Slime; shiny ingrained dirt.

gloaming
Dusk; twilight; sunset. (See also: dailigone.)

gobshite
A fool; someone who talks rubbish.

go canny
Go carefully; be alert.

going-away coat
It was customary for a bridal couple, after the wedding feast, to leave to go on their honeymoon. The bride changed out of her wedding dress into her 'going-away' clothes.

gombeen-man
Contemptuous term for a shopkeeper or trader who is interested only in making money; an unscrupulous profiteer; shady businessman who makes a profit at someone's else's expense; moneylender who charges exorbitant interest.

goose's wing
When the goose or turkey was killed at Christmas, part of a wing with the feathers on it was retained. These long, strong feathers made the wing into a very useful duster which would be used to sweep flour from a bakeboard or griddle, or dust the ash from the top of a stove.

gorget
A patch of colouring on the throat of a bird; a garment that covers the throat.

gowling
Howling; yelling; bellowing; roaring.

grags, bog-fir grags
Withered tree stumps.

graith, war-graith
Equipment; apparel; gear; wealth; horse harness.

griddle
A flat, usually round, cast-iron pan on which soda and wheaten bread, potato bread and pancakes were cooked. It had a hooped handle to enable it to be slung on a crane over an open fire. More often in recent years, it would be employed on the top of a range or cooker.

grocery cart
Grocery shops would send a cart,
later a motor van, around the
local countryside, selling groceries
to people who rarely got to town.

gully knife
A large sharp kitchen knife;
originally the knife used to kill a
pig, by cutting its gullet.

gumption
Sense; having common sense;
reliable; showing initiative; being
resourceful.

guttery
Wet; muddy; filthy.

...H...

habergeon
Part of chainmail armour;
sleeveless coat of armour.

hackled
Combed flax with a hackle, a type
of steel comb.

haft
Handle of an implement.

haggard
A sheltered spot near the
farmyard where stacks of hay were
kept during the winter. It made it
more convenient for the farmer
getting fodder for the livestock,
which overwintered inside. Stacks
of corn could be kept there too,
waiting to be threshed.

hagged
Hacked; cut.

half-door
A half door is an external
door which is divided in two
horizontally. The two halves can
be opened independently. It
was in common use and had a
practical purpose. When the top
half was open and the bottom
half closed, fresh air could
enter, but not the fowl in the
farmyard. Toddlers were kept
safely indoors, and it was easy to
throw a crust to the dog, scraps
to the hens or throw out a basin
of dirty water.

hames
A mess. To make a hames of
something is to mess it up; get
it wrong; make a hash of it;
or muddle it. A hames is also
part of draught horse's harness,
attached to the collar.

hammer and tongs
To go at something with furious
energy; to go at something
with great vigour, violence or
enthusiasm.

skittering his spit
Pipe smokers and tobacco chewers sometimes spat excess saliva into the fire, or in the direction of the fire. If it landed on the stove top it danced in little bubbles across it before drying up.

slabbering, slabbery
Drooling; wetting; dripping.

sledge
A sledgehammer has a large, flat metal head. The hammer is used for jobs requiring a great deal of force such as driving in fence posts or breaking rocks.

sledgehead
The head of a sledgehammer.

sleekit
Sly; slippery; untrustworthy; ingratiating.

sleepers
Wooden blocks laid to support a railway line.

slobber
(n) Muck; mud; mire; (v) to drool; to let liquid or saliva drip from the mouth; to gush.

slubbed
Twisted; irregular.

slugged
Slapped heavily.

smack hands and sell
On fair days when a bargain was struck, and a beast sold, the buyer and seller would slap hands, palm to palm, sometimes spitting first on the hand. This sealed the bargain. It was customary too when the actual cash was handed over for the seller to hand back a little of the money, a 'luck penny'.

smart
Sting with a sharp pain.

smit
Give disease to someone else; infect.

smithereens
Small pieces; fragments.

smoke-reek
Strong smell of smoke.

smoothing iron
A domestic implement; an iron heated and used to remove creases from clothes.

snares
Rabbit snares were made of wire. A loop of wire, attached firmly to a piece of wood stuck into the ground, would be set on a path regularly used by rabbits. The snare would be set at rabbit-head-height so that the rabbit's head would be caught in the loop.

snedder
Someone who cuts the leaves and roots off a turnip.

snotters
Mucus coming from the nose.

snottery
The sound of mucus being sucked back up the nostrils. A snottery person is unpleasant; awkward; arrogant.

soda farl
Soda bread is made with flour, salt, baking soda and buttermilk. When the mixed bread is flattened into a circle on a floured board and then cut in four, each quarter is called a farl. Soda farls are cooked on a griddle.

sogs
Soaks.

sorry for my trouble
When visiting a wake house it is customary to shake hands with each relative of the deceased person saying, "I'm sorry for your trouble."

sough
A moaning, whistling, rushing sound, a sound made by the wind in trees.

splay-foot
A broad flat foot; a foot with low arches; a foot that splays outwards when walking.

sporran
Part of Highland dress – a small pouch, which hangs at the front of the kilt.

spray potatoes
Spray potatoes with bluestone to prevent blight.

spreadfield
The bog; ground where turf is spread to dry.

spree
A pleasurable outing; a period of unrestrained activity.

spring-well
A well sunk where a spring of water comes out of the ground.

spud of the dynamo
A dynamo was used to power the lights on a bicycle. It was powered by the movement of the wheels as the cyclist pedalled. It would not be needed during the day so the spud was pulled back.

stacks
When grass was cut for hay it was traditionally shaken and turned till it was dry. It was then piled into

stacks and tramped down until the hay was firm. These stacks were beehive-shaped structures, tied down with hay ropes to ensure the hay did not blow away.

staff
A stick; a walking stick; a stick with a special use e.g. that used in churning.

stall-chains
The chains used to keep cattle in their stalls, their particular place in the byre.

stays
Corsets; garments designed to support the back and pull in the waist. They were often stiffened with whalebone.

steadfast
Loyal; resolute; unwavering; resisted attack.

still
Part of the apparatus used to distil whiskey; used in the production of illegal spirits such as poteen.

stone-walled
Sometimes fields were delineated by walls rather than hedges. These walls were commonly built from stones which had been lifted when the field was being cleared.

stood my ground
Did not waver; stood up for my rights.

stooks, stooked corn
When grain was cut it was tied into sheaves. These were stood up in threes, balancing against each other. These formations were called stooks.

stour
Dust; moving dust, e.g. when feet move on dusty floorboards or a person or a vehicle moves along a dusty road.

stout
A dark beer made with hops, water, yeast and roasted malt. Guinness is the best-known stout in Ireland.

straw-must
Mould; dust.

streel-haired
Untidy; slovenly.

stubbed
Used an implement such as a stubbing knife (machete) to clear land by removing roots and tree stumps.

súgán
A straw or hay rope used to cover a rick or stack of hay or grain to

help them keep their shape and prevent the hay or straw being blown away.

sup
Small mouthful; sip.

swinged, swinged the land
Struck hard; beat down; laid waste; scourged.

...T...

tar border
A strip of tar painted at ground level along a whitewashed wall. It looked good and helped preserve the whitewash and repel mildew.

tea-chest
A deep-sided, foil-lined wooden box in which loose tealeaves were packed. Grocers weighed the tealeaves into bags for customers. The empty chests were useful for storing things and many a house had one. They had numerous uses, for example, to keep bedding tidy, to hold pork being salted for bacon or to house a clocking hen.

teem
To pour; to rain heavily; to pour water off boiled potatoes.

tetter-barked
A skin disease marked by white areas or eruption; an itchy condition of the skin.

thane
The chief of a clan. A person who has been granted lands; king's attendant at court; owner of a manor house; a royal official.

thatch
Covering the roof with reeds, rushes or straw. The vegetation is tightly packed and layered so as well as keeping out rain, it provides some insulation. Good quality straw thatch can last for several decades.

thatcher
A person who puts a thatch roof on a building. It is a skilled job.

the book
The Bible.

thick-witted
Slow thinking, stupid; dull.

thole
Tolerate; endure; put up with; suffer.

thorn tree/fairy thorn
It was believed some thorn trees were under the protection of the fairies or little folk. Bad luck

would come to anyone who cut
down a fairy thorn.

thornproof
A thick durable tweed material
made from double-twisted yarn,
which thorns cannot penetrate.

thrawn
Awkward; argumentative;
contrary; stubborn.

thresh, threshed corn
To separate the grain from the
stalks.

thresher
A machine which threshes grain.

throughother
Untidy; disordered, confused,
mind unclear.

thrum/thrumming
A repetitive strumming; a monot-
onous beat. Making a continuous
rhythmic humming sound.

tinsmith
Sometimes also called a tinker –
a person who makes or mends
articles made of tin.

tin whistle
Also called the penny whistle, it
is a type of flute, like a recorder.
It is often used to play Irish
traditional music.

tongs
An instrument with two movable
arms that are joined at one end,
used for picking up and holding
things; an implement used to
add, remove or arrange coal or
turf on a fire.

tongue-and-groove
A method of fitting wood
together edge to edge to make
a strong joint and a single flat
surface.

topgallant
One of the sails above the
topmast on a sailing ship.

torques
A piece of personal adornment
consisting of a ring of precious
metal, open at one end. It is worn
around the neck. A torque was
usually made of gold, silver or
bronze.

tow
A course fibre produced during
the scutching of lint. It is pale
in colour and can be used in
the production of paper and for
stuffing upholstery.

townland
All of Ireland is divided into
townlands, small geographical
divisions, each with its own
name. The name of the townland

generally indicates something about its topography or history or gives the names of the families who lived there.

traces
The part of a horse's harness made of straps or chains. The traces are used to take the pull from the breastcollar or hames. (See also: hames.)

trig
Spruce; tidy; trim.

trindle
Wheel, roll, trundle.

trundle
Move slowly and heavily.

turf/peat
Partially decayed compressed vegetable matter found in bogs or wetlands. It can be cut into slabs, dried and used as fuel.

turfbanks
The areas in the bog or moss where turf is cut.

turf clod
A small dried lump of turf.

turf coom(-b)
Debris of turf left on the ground when a turf stack has been used up. Coomb can be used to spread

in a byre or animal house to soak up manure.

turf dust
Dust of turf left on the ground when a turf stack has been used up.

turf mould
Fine dust or particles of turf left on the ground when a turf stack has been used up; coom(-b).

turfsmoke
Smoke from a turf fire. It has a distinctive, pleasant smell.

turf-spade
A special implement for cutting turf out of the bog.

turf stack
A stack of turf often built against the gable wall of a house. The sods were angled to allow rain to run off them. Some stacks had a hollow where the dog slept.

turnhole
A bend in a river where the water is fast flowing.

turnip-man
A jack-o'-lantern. A turnip is hollowed, a face carved on it and a lighted candle placed inside.

twang
Accent.

two arms the one length
Having nothing with you. A person said to have two arms the one length is someone who has not brought a gift when one is expected.

uisquebaugh
From the Irish 'uisce beatha', literally meaning 'the water of life', more commonly known as whiskey.

wain
A wagon or chariot.

wake/wake house
A vigil held in the house of someone who has died – in the corpse (or corp) house. Relatives, friends and neighbours come and go over the two or three days between the death and funeral.

wallstead
A ruined building, with only the walls left standing.

war-graith
Armour.

wean
A wee one; child.

wee
Small.

welted
With raised marks; ribbed; with weals/swollen marks on it.

'wet grass bleached our boots'
Boots were made of leather and when they got very wet the dye was bleached out of them. This could be restored by applying shoe polish, in the appropriate colour, to the leather. If the boots were very wet they would be stuffed with newspaper and left by the fire to dry.

wheep
A short, sharp cry.

wheesht!, hold your wheesht!
A command to be quiet.

whet
Sharpen.

whins
Furze; gorse. Whin bushes produce bright yellow blossom with a coconut scent. Whin blossom is used to dye hard boiled eggs at Easter. There is

blossom on whin bushes all year round, although it is more lavish in spring and summer, and has led to the old saying: 'Kissing's (or courting's) out of season when the whin is out of bloom.'

whinge
Whine, complain, persistent moaning about something.

whinged
Whined, complained.

whinny, whinny ground
Covered with whins, furze; rough ground.

whiskey muddler
A tool used in creating drinks. It could be used like a pestle to crush fruit or herbs into a drink or it could be used to stir a drink. In a hot whiskey, a muddler would be used to stir the lemon, sugar and cloves into the drink.

whitewash
(n) Walls, mainly the exterior walls, of houses were covered with a mixture of lime and water. This was cheap and dried quickly to a bright white. It was mildly antibacterial. Sometimes a contrasting border of tar was painted along the bottom of the walls. (See also: tar border.)
(v) To cover up something unpleasant; to make something sound more palatable; to deceive.

whitewash brush
A brush with long flexible bristles, used to apply whitewash.

wicker creels
When potatoes were dug, they were gathered first into wicker baskets. These were then carried to the side of the field and the potatoes emptied out of them into potato pits. (See also: potato pits.)

Williamite cannon
A cannon used in the battles between King James II and King William of Orange.

winkers
Part of a horse's harness. Like a blinker it is a piece of leather sewn onto the harness to prevent the horse seeing what is on either side. The horse can only look straight ahead.

wintering out
Keeping livestock out of doors during the winter.

wishing tree
A specific tree which is credited with a spiritual value or powers of healing. Those visiting the tree go with a particular intention in mind and usually leave an

offering. This could be a coin
pushed into the bark of the tree
or a rag tied to a branch.

wood-kerne
Kernes were light-armed Irish
foot soldiers. Wood-kernes were
guerrilla fighters who lived in the
woods of Ireland.

wraith
An apparition, or ghost-like
figure, of someone seen usually
before but sometimes after, their
death.

yellow boots
Light brown /yellowish laced
boots traditionally worn by cattle
dealers.

your side of the house
Your religion. In Northern
Ireland this usually means
Catholic or Protestant.

you've done your station
You've done your share of
suffering. Do your station –
literally do the penance of
a pilgrimage to St Patrick's
Purgatory on Lough Derg.

St Tida's Church, on Church Island, Lough
Beg, site of an ancient monastic settlement
established by St Patrick in the 5th century.
(Photograph by Joe McAllister.)

Seamus Heaney wrote the poem 'The Strand at Lough Beg' in memory of his cousin, Colum McCartney.

The lough shore at New Ferry, Bellaghy.

Listening to the river in
the trees, South Derry.

Reeds, such as these growing on Lough Beg,
are used to make Brigid's crosses.

The graveyard at St Mary's
Parish Church, Bellaghy
where Seamus Heaney is
buried, close to his parents.

The church and graveyard are overlooked by sycamore trees.

Seamus Heaney's epitaph is a quotation from his poem 'The Gravel Walks', published in his 1996 collection 'The Spirit Level'.

Writer Maura Johnston pictured beside the portrait of Seamus Heaney by Jeffrey Morgan, which hangs at the HomePlace in Bellaghy.

David Annand's sculpture 'The Turf Man' at Bellaghy Bawn, which honours Seamus Heaney's poem 'Digging'.

PART TWO

Deeper Roots

THRESHING

The hum and gulp of the thresher ran down
And the big belt slew to a standstill
The Wife's Tale

Threshing took place in autumn. It was a noisy process. A threshing machine separated grain – corn, wheat, oats – from stalks and husks. The stooks of grain would be brought to the thresher. A stook was made up of three sheaves leaning against each other.Someone would pierce a sheaf with a pitchfork and toss it to another man who fed it into the thresher.

The threshing machine was attached by a fan to a tractor engine, and did its work of separation. Straw was ejected at one end, grain at the other and the husks or chaff fell to the ground. The straw was stacked or sometimes fed into a baler. The grain poured into sacks. These were fastened at the side of the thresher and the men there had to be quick to remove a full bag and fasten on an empty sack.

The husks, the outer part of the grain, was known as chaff. It was usually burned but could be used to stuff mattresses.

The man who owned the threshing machine would go around the countryside, travelling from farm to farm. When the thresher was due, a farmer would notify the neighbours and they would come to help, as it took several men to operate the thresher. In turn the farmer would help at other farms. This system of voluntary labour was known as morrowing.

CHURNING

Out came the four crocks, spilled their heavy lip
of cream, their white insides, into the sterile churn.
Churning Day

Churning – turning milk into butter. When cows were milked, the milk was poured into a crock or crocks. A crock is an earthenware container with a glazed interior. The milk was left to settle for a day or two. The cream was skimmed off and put in the churn.

A churn used to be a wooden barrel- like container with a hole in the lid through which a wooden pole or staff could be inserted. This was moved rapidly up and down to agitate the milk. It was hard work and often several people took turns to move the staff, or 'take a plunge'.

If it was taking a long time for the butter to come, sometimes a little boiling water was added – but only a little. Too much would make the butter pale.

Churning stopped when little clumps of butter, little yellow grains, began to form. The churn was opened and the butter removed. What remained in the churn was buttermilk. This was a favourite drink to accompany dinner or to relieve thirst of workers in the field or to make soda bread.

The butter was then put in a bowl, traditionally a wooden bowl. The butter was washed in several changes of cold water to remove the last of the buttermilk. Then a knife was passed through it several times, criss-cross, to remove any hairs from the cow or other impurities.

Salt was added at this stage and thoroughly mixed in. The butter as then shaped into rectangular blocks or little balls, using butter spades. Sometimes a butter print was pressed on the block of butter to make a design.

BREAD BAKING

So, her hands scuffled
over the bakeboard,
the reddening stove

sent its plaque of heat
against her where she stood
in a floury apron
by the window.
Mossbawn Sunlight

In Irish bread making, yeast was rarely used. The raising agent was bicarbonate of soda, commonly called baking soda. It worked with buttermilk to make the bread rise.

The ingredients of soda bread are: plain flour, salt, soda and buttermilk. These are mixed together to a soft, but not sticky, dough and kneaded very briefly on a floured surface, usually a board kept especially for this, the bakeboard. The bread can then be formed into a round, the surface scored with a cross and baked in the oven. Or the dough can be flattened with the hand into a circle. This can be cut into four and the resulting farls baked on a hot, dry griddle.

The basic dough can be varied by adding wheatmeal, yellow meal or a handful of mixed dried fruit. Sometimes a little ground ginger is added and treacle stirred into the buttermilk before it is added. Another way is to put half the dough, slightly flattened, on a baking tray, add a layer of sliced, sugared apples and top with another layer of bread dough before baking. Nowadays people add herbs, dried tomatoes, seaweeds, seeds, sundried tomatoes...

Recipe for soda bread
Ingredients
450g plain flour,
1 level teaspoon baking soda,
1 level teaspoon salt,
about 350ml buttermilk

Method

Heat the oven to about 180. Put the baking soda in the palm of one hand and rub with the fingers of the other to remove any lumps. Add it to the salt and flour in a bowl. Mix well. Pour in most of the buttermilk and stir well. Add more milk, if necessary, until a soft dough is formed. Turn out onto a well floured surface. Pat and shape it into a round. Flatten with your palms until it is 2.5cm thick. Put on a floured baking tray. Score a cross on the surface. Bake for 40–45 minutes. It is cooked when the bread is browned on top and sounds hollow when tapped on the bottom.

Potato bread is another favourite in Ireland. Potatoes, these can be leftovers from dinner, are mashed with salt. Plain flour is mixed in to form a stiff dough. This is flattened, or rolled, on a floured surface, cut into rounds or triangles and cooked on a hot floured griddle. It can be eaten hot, with plenty of butter, or fried with bacon, sausage or eggs.

LINEN PRODUCTION

All year the flax-dam festered in the heart
Of the townland; green and heavy headed
Flax had rotted there, weighted down by huge sods.
Death of a Naturalist

Linen production used to be Ireland's staple industry. Linen is a fabric made from flax. Flax seed is sown in May and the plants can grow to a metre high. The fibres which grow the length of the stem help to hold it up. Flax produces a little blue flower and in the heyday of flax growing in Ireland there were so many fields of it that people said it was as if the sky had fallen.

Flax, also called lint, was harvested in August, a back-breaking and labour-intensive job. It was not cut, because that would have damaged the fibres. It was pulled from the ground by hand – lint pulling. Four handfuls were bundled together into a sheaf called a beet. This was tied with a band made from rushes.

Then came the unpleasant part of the process. The pectins holding the fibres to the stem had to be dissolved without breaking the fibres. They were rotted, or retted, away. Farmers would dam part of a stream or ditch. This was the lint hole. The beets of lint were put head down in the water and weighed down with stones or sods. The lint was left there to rot for about eight days. The stench of this retting process was overpowering and could be smelled over a large area.

After retting was completed, the beets had to lifted out of the stagnant water and spread on the banks to dry. This was nasty work and those involved in it would be encouraged when they went home to strip off their clothes, wash themselves and then enter the house in fresh clothes, leaving the ill-smelling garments outside.

The lint was spread to dry, then retied in beets. These were propped together in pairs until really dry. The beets were then taken to a scutch mill which extracted the fibres. The outer woody stalk was broken into pieces called shous, often used as fuel in household fires.

Then came hackling where the fibre was combed again and again. Waste fibre was known as tow, and used for stuffing mattresses and furniture. The longer fibres were spun into thread which in turn was woven into linen.

SAVING TURF

My grandfather cut more turf in a day
Than any other man on Toner's bog.
Digging

Turf or peat, was used extensively as household fuel. It is made up of partially decomposed vegetation that has been pressed in the ground for thousands of years.

The area where the turf is cut is known as the bog or the moss. Although today turf is cut by machine, for hundreds of years it was cut by hand, using a two bladed spade, called a slean, out of a turf bank. This spade cut the turf into neat rectangles. These were tossed onto the ground by the bank and spread to dry on an area known as the spreadfield.

When it was dry enough to handle, the turf was footed. This meant standing several of the sods on end, leaning against each other. This meant the wind could blow through the spaces and speed the drying process.

When the turf was dry it was built into larger piles called clamps or ricks and stayed there until it was time to transport it home. Here it was built in a long narrow stack, shaped so the rain ran off it, or stored in a shed.

Saving turf was hard work, but enjoyable. It was labour intensive and, like threshing or pulling flax, morrowing, the sharing of voluntary labour, was useful. Many people have happy memories of days spent on the moss. The weather had to be dry, was often sunny. There was good company. Tea was made and eggs boiled in cans hung over turf fires.

Burning turf has an aroma which most people find pleasant.

THE FAIR DAY

Even a solid man,
A pillar to himself and to his trade,
All yellow boots and stick and soft felt hat
Can sprout wings at the ankle and grow fleet
As the god of fair days ...
Crossings xxvii

The date of the local fair day was important in the rural community up until the 1960's. Most fair-sized towns and villages had their fair day. It was a set date e.g. the 21st of the month (or the following day if that date fell on a Sunday), or a particular day, say the second Tuesday of the month.

On the fair day, cattle, sheep and horses were walked to the fair, the farmer guiding and prodding them with his ashplant. Pigs were usually on a cart or in a trailer. Manys a farmer's wife would scrub the little pigs with soapsuds to make them look their best when they were reclining on straw at the fair.

In the town there was usually a grassy area, normally called the Fair Hill, where the livestock could be herded and displayed. Along the main street there would also be animals on show. Shops would put barricades across their windows to prevent the glass being broken by a runaway beast. Children were often given the day off school.

Buyers would wander around inspecting animals, feeling their sides, their udders. In the case of horses, teeth would be examined and the seller would be asked to trot the animal up and down so a prospective buyer could see its gait.

Dealing was done face to face, and it was a matter of principle to bargain. The seller would name a price. The buyer would say what he was prepared to pay, usually much lower. So they argued and the figure would go up and down until the buyer would offer nothing higher and the seller would not accept that amount. Then one of the bystanders would urge them to 'split the difference' and that would be done – the discrepancy divided in two.

The deal was sealed when one of the men would spit on his hand and the two men shook hands. Then the seller would pass to the buyer some coins as a 'luck penny'. The buyer had to make his own arrangements to get the animal home.

With the fair day came itinerant singers; stalls selling confectionery or ropes, or nails, or farming implements would be set up. A travelling dentist sometimes came too. There might be eggs or grass seed, cabbage plants or live poultry for sale – depending on the time of year.

Enterprising women would throw open their front room and sell food. The offerings were a plain tea – tea and buttered soda bread - or a meat tea. This had the addition of stewed meat and gravy. And of course pubs did a roaring trade with men offering each other 'a treat' especially to celebrate the successful conclusion of a sale.

A fair day brought bustle and money and the opportunity to catch up on the local news. When he got home the farmer was invariably asked, "Was there many at the fair?"

BLACKBERRY PICKING

Then red ones inked up and that hunger
Sent us out with milk cans, pea tins, jam-pots
Where briars scratched and wet grass bleached our boots.
Round hayfields, cornfields and potato-drills
We trekked and picked until the cans were full
Blackberry Picking

Picking blackberries was important in the lives of rural children. Blackberries were commonplace in the hedges – and there were more hedges and smaller fields then too! Of course children picked them to eat. Or their mothers or grannies may have included them in apple tarts and crumbles. They may even have been made into bramble jelly – with the addition of crab apples to help the jelly set. Crab apples are little yellow or red apples which grow wild and are too sour to eat.

But the main reason for picking blackberries was to sell them. No-one enquired why they were bought; it was assumed for dye. A man in a van might come to collect the berries, or sometimes the agent was a local shopkeeper and the berries could be taken there. The berries were weighed and paid for by the pound. The money thus earned was useful. The children might get keeping some of it, but the cash was frequently used to buy winter boots or clothes. So one can understand why Seamus Heaney felt sad when the fruit rotted.

'*Wet grass bleached our boots*'
Boots were made of leather and when they got wet, the colour was bleached out of them. This could be restored by using shoe polish on the leather. If the boots were very wet, they would be stuffed with newspaper and left by the fire to dry.

WAKES

I was embarrassed
By old men standing up to shake my hand
And tell me they were 'sorry for my trouble'.
Mid-Term Break

Holding a wake is an important rite of passage in Irish culture. A burial takes place usually on the third day after a person dies. During the days between death and burial the wake is held.

Holding a wake is a long-established tradition in Ireland and exists in some form or another today. It normally takes place in the home of the deceased or in that of a relative. In some localities this house will be referred to as 'the corp house', or 'the corpse house'.

Immediately after a death, a window is opened to let the spirit escape. The corpse is laid out on the bed or, more usually in an open coffin. A family member usually sits nearby. It was customary, and still happens in some areas, for the corpse never to be left unattended from death until the funeral. Quite often neighbouring men would volunteer to 'sit up' and would stay in the room all night. This gave the family time to rest. These men would talk, tell stories and perhaps sing.

A tradition which has died out almost everywhere is the tradition of the keening women. There were women, sometimes paid, who would cry and keen over the dead body, singing praises and lamenting the fact of the death. This took place when the body was laid out and again at the funeral.

The corpse is dressed in its best clothes. In Catholic families rosary beads may be entwined in its hands. In Protestant homes a Bible may be laid on the corpse or displayed nearby.

There will be lit candles nearby and, again in Catholic homes, a dish of holy water. A sprig of greenery will be in this and mourners can use this to sprinkle holy water on the deceased. The coffin lid will be propped against the wall, the brass plaque giving the name of the dead person and the date of death.

Sometimes all clocks are stopped at the time of death, and not restarted until after the funeral. All curtains will be drawn so the house is dimly lit.

Mirrors will be covered with white cloths. Various reasons are given for this custom including the idea that one is not distracted , by gazing at one's reflection, from mourning. Or that at the time of a death evil spirits come to the house and can be seen reflected in a mirror.

As the news of the death spreads by word of mouth, or when the death notice is read in a local paper, people start coming to the house. It is customary when admitted to the house, to, as you come across them, shake the hands of all the relations of the deceased person and say, "Sorry for your trouble."

You will be asked if you'd like to see the corpse, led to it. It is usual to stand for a little while looking at the body and perhaps saying a prayer. Then, if you feel like it, you may touch or kiss the corpse. It is usual to comment on how the deceased is looking and to hear of the events leading to the death.

At this point you move away to leave room for someone else to come to the coffin. You will be offered a chair in another room. Tea, sandwiches, biscuits and cakes will be offered. Alcohol, cigarettes, snuff, clay pipes and tobacco used to be provided, but this is rarely done today.

Now is the time for talking. The death and its circumstances will be commented on. Stories involving the deceased will be related. Jokes may be told. General conversation will ensue.

When you feel like going you will probably ascertain the funeral arrangements and again offer sympathy.

The wake celebrates the life of the person who has died. It is a way to bind the living and the dead and to contemplate the inevitability of death itself. Death is the portal to an afterlife, so it is a time for celebration.

TOWNLANDS

All year the flax-dam festered in the heart
Of the townland; green and heavy headed
Flax had rotted there, weighted down by huge sods.
Death of a Naturalist

In any consideration of the regions of Ireland, townlands must feature. Ireland was traditionally divided into baronies, baronies into parishes.

But regions known as townlands existed before parishes or counties, and were created for easier administration of the country.

From the 17th century land was let by landlords on a townland basis, and rent, tithe, census and valuation books all used townlands as distinct units.

Townlands range in size from a few acres to several thousand.

There are around 62,000 townlands in Ireland.

Each townland has its own name. The name could derive from a local family name, from the topography of the area or from an important event which took place there.

People are generally proud of, and loyal to, their own townland.

Many of the names of townlands are derived from the Irish language, and can reflect the history or the type of land usage in the area in days gone by.

Useful words to know when translating townland names are: 'mor' (big); 'beg' (small); 'bally' (town). Prefixes such as 'dun' (fort), 'gort' (tilled field), 'cil' (church) are examples of words which are also common.

Townlands around Bellaghy

Bellaghy: the mouth or entrance to the marshy place

East Glebe: Glebe lands i.e. land belonging to the church

West Glebe: see above

Ballyscullion West: the townland of the O'Scullions

Drumanee Lower: The hill ridge of the deer

Old Town Deer Park: the castle was in oldtown Deer park

Ballydermot: town or townland of the Dermots

Church Island Intake: Inis-Toide (after St Toit)

Edenreagh: The grey brow or face of the hill

Kilberry: The woods of the Berrys

Kilberry Downing: The woods of the Berrys – named after the Downing family

Kilberry Boyd: after the Boyd family

Old Town Downing: called after the Downing family

Mullaghboy: The yellow hill or hill top

Tamlaghtduff: The black plague monument

Drumlamph: The ridge of the elm trees

Broagh: The brink or edge of the river

Tamniaran: the field or residence of the O'Harans

Leitrim: The grey hill ridge

Rocktown: The rocky district

Ballymacombs Mor: Townland of the Macombs – big

Ballymacombs Beg: Townland of the Macombs – small

Ballymacpeake Upper: The town or townland of the McPeakes

Drumard: The high ridge

Ballynease: The townland of the Aengus

Lemnaroy: The leap of the red horse

Anahorish: Place of clear water, is part of the townland of *Creagh*: The shaking bog

CURES

Believe in miracles
And cures and healing wells.
The Cure at Troy

Some people try to cure themselves of ailments. Many cures use local plants and household ingredients. For a common cold, take punch i.e. hot whiskey with sugar, cloves and lemon.

A sore throat will at least be eased by sipping, either hot or cold, a mixture of honey, lemons and ginger. Whiskey may be added. A sock filled with hot salt and wrapped round the neck may also relieve a sore throat.

Ground ginger dissolved in hot milk might be taken for indigestion or an upset stomach. A daily spoonful of honey produced by local bees will mitigate the effects of hay fever. Nettle juice or nettle soup will help cure arthritis or anaemia.

Fasting spittle i.e. saliva spat out before you have breakfasted, will cure warts. Or if you cut a potato, rub warts with the cut edge, then throw the potato away, the warts will leave as the potato rots.

And for generations the Irish have believed that some special people have 'the cure'. This means they have the ability to cure without resort to conventional medicine. It is based on a belief that religious or magical thinking, sometimes with herbs or potions, and sometimes with specific actions, can effect a cure.

The seventh son of a seventh son is believed to have the cure; if two people having the same surname marry, they will have the cure; sometimes the ability to cure is passed down from one member of a family to another.

Each cure is for a specific ailment for example warts, chicken pox, haemorrhoids, whooping cough, sprains, shingles.

A child with whooping cough would be passed three times over and under a donkey. One cure for a sprain is to hold a piece of thread between your palms while prayers are said.

Shingles could be cured by touching the afflicted part with a sprig of holly and saying a prayer. A stye on the eye would disappear after being pricked with the thorn from a gooseberry bush and saying prayers. The cure can be used on animals.

The person with the cure does not advertise. People find out by word of mouth. Nor will the healer accept payment and, in some cases, the patient is not even to say, "Thank you". And there is no need to physically meet. A cure may be asked for by a third party or in a telephone conversation.

Healing wells

There are roughly 3000 healing or holy wells in Ireland. They were usually sunk where a natural spring occurs. Healing wells have been around since prehistoric times and may have marked the sites for pagan sacrifice. Some were taken over by the Christian church and have been given saints' names and become holy wells.

The belief is still strong in many parts of Ireland that a person with an ailment who bathes in these wells, drinks water from them or rubs the water on the afflicted part will be cured. Some wells have the power to cure a specific condition – warts, epilepsy, infertility.

Bullauns may be found near healing wells. A bullaun is a stone with part of its surface hollowed out. The water which collects in this hollow is said to have healing properties.

In pagan Ireland special visits were made to these wells on February 1st, May 1st, August 1st and November 1st. Nowadays these visits, or patterns, take place on the feast day of the saint after whom the well is named. These patterns include prayer and walking, in the direction in which the sun moves, around the well.

When choosing the site for the well, spring water was essential, but there was often a tree nearby, which was sacred. When a pilgrim bathed, washed or drank at the well, the cloth used or a rag or a piece of clothing was tied to the tree. This would bear your illness. As the cloth rotted away, so the ailment disappeared. Some people pressed pins or small coins into the bark of the tree, or threw them into the well as an offering.

THE BANSHEE AND FAIRY FOLK

The banshee acoustic
Of the glass-and-iron dome upping the wildness.
Red, White and Blue

The banshee, literally fairy woman, bean sidhe, is a being which wails or shrieks to warn of a death. She is particularly associated with families whose surnames begin with O or Mc.

She can be heard at night but is rarely seen. She can apparently look like a beautiful young woman or an ugly old one. She invariably wears a grey or white hooded cloak. She has long grey hair which she combs and her eyes are red from crying.

The banshee is not to be confused with a wraith. A wraith also heralds a death. It is a ghostlike image of someone and would be seen shortly before that person's death. It is possible to see the wraith of a family member who lives far away or in another country.

Irish people treat their fairies, the little people, the good people, with respect. Dirty washing up would not be thrown out the door in case it hit a little person. They are very fastidious and are likely to seek revenge. But if clean water is left out for them, they will return this kindness with blessings.

They have been known to abduct a healthy baby and substitute a weakly, sickly one. This baby is known as a changeling. Or as punishment for cutting down a tree in the middle of a field, a whitethorn tree, known as a fairy thorn, the person who cuts the tree will soon after meet with an accident, or even death.

The tree guards the entry to the otherworld which the little folk inhabit. The good people also live in raths or hill forts.

On May Day fairies are particularly active. Steps can be taken to protect a house and livestock. Flowers such as primroses, whin blossom and hawthorn could be placed on doorsteps or door posts, across the byre door or across the horns of cows to keep away evil.

Leprechauns are mischievous people who will lure a person with the promise of gold and will always outwit the human.

The banshee is one of the good people, but one who is dreaded and feared.

The Lambeg drum, one of the loudest acoustic instruments, mainly used by Orangemen, though also by some Hibernian bands.

A crock – earthenware with a glazed interior. Used to hold
drinking water from the well or milk.

The Conway Stewart fountain pen was a treasured
possession and a big advance on the 'dip' pen.

Brigid's crosses are made from rushes to celebrate the feast of the saint on February 1. Also pictured is an oaten scone, traditionally eaten on St Brigid's Day.

A billhook is traditionally used for cutting shrubs
and other small woody material.

Butter spades, used to form butter into pounds,
half-pounds and little balls.

A creamery can, used to transport milk from the farm to the creamery.

Traditional milk churns were made of wood. The lid had a hole
in it through which went a plunger, or dasher. This was moved up
and down till the butter was formed.

A door latch.

Whin bushes grow wild on bogland in South Derry,
producing yellow blossoms with a coconut scent.

A griddle of potato bread.

Soda bread is made with flour, salt, baking soda and
buttermilk and traditionally cooked on a griddle.

A harvest bow.

A turf-spade, also known as a sleán, is used for cutting turf from a bog.

Turf being dug up from the bog (above),
is often stacked in clods for drying (below).

A field of flax in bloom.

A stook of flax beets (sheaves).

Edge of an ancient fort, Tullyhogue.

A thatched roof.

Hurricane lamps.

INDEX OF HEARTH LANGUAGE

In compiling this glossary, it has become apparent that the list of 'hearth' terms requiring definition will grow as words fall out of common usage. In an attempt to future-proof the index, we have constructed the index to allow for new insertions. The specific Seamus Heaney publications referenced in this glossary are:

Death of a Naturalist (1966) – DN

Door into the Dark (1969) – DD

Wintering Out (1972) – WO

North (1975) – NH

Field Work (1979) – FW

Sweeney Astray (1983) – SA

Station Island (1984) – SI

The Haw Lantern (1987) – HL

The Cure at Troy (1990) – CT

Seeing Things (1991) – ST

The Spirit Level (1996) – SL

Beowulf (1999) – BF

Electric Light (2001) – EL

The Burial at Thebes (2004) – CT

District and Circle (2006) – DC

The Testament of Cresseid and Seven Fables (2009) – TF

Human Chain (2010) – HC

Aeneid Book VI (2016) – AB

DEATH OF A NATURALIST (1966): DN

1 **Digging** – turf, bog, potato mould, peat
2 **Death of a Naturalist** – flax-dam, townland, slobber
3 **The Barn** – threshed corn, chaff, two-lugged, plough-socks, scythe, pitch fork
4 **An Advancement of Learning** – hen-coop
5 **Blackberry-Picking** – milk-cans, briars, byre, bath
6 **Churning Day** – crocks, churn, staff, whiskey muddler, slugged, flabby, butter-spades, plash
7 **The Early Purges** – pump, dunghill, dung
8 **Follower** – headrig
9 **Ancestral Photograph** – heckled, smack hands and sell, fairs, fair days
10 **Mid-Term Break** – sorry for my trouble
11 **Dawn Shoot** – sleepers, cudding, whins, whitewash, playboy, dandered, cut out the tongue
12 **At a Potato Digging** – wicker creels, pit, 'forty-five, blighted root
13 **For the Commander of the Eliza** – creek, bia
14 **The Diviner** – diviner
16 **Cow in Calf** – byre
18 **Waterfall** – the burn
19 **Docker** – sledgehead, Roman collar, porter, Celtic cross
24 **Lovers on Aran** – Aran
25 **Poem (for Marie)** – clabber
28 **Storm on the Island** – hay, stacks, stooks
29 **Synge on Aran** – keening
31 **In Small Townlands** – hogshair wedge
33 **The Play Way** – milk-tops, snares

DOOR INTO THE DARK (1969): DD

2 **Gone** – bellyband, blinkers, traces, reek, shods, reek

3 **Dream** – billhook

4 **The Outlaw** – ash-plant

7 **Thatcher** – thatcher

8 **The Peninsula** – Whitewash

9 **In Gallarus Oratory** – turfstack, barrow

11 **Requiem for the Croppies** – Croppies, pike

13 **Undine** – right of way, briars

14 **The Wife's Tale** – thresher, forks - pitchforks

17 **Elegy for a Stillborn Child** – creel

18 **Victorian Guitar** – stays

20 **At Ardboe Point** – chaff

22 **A Lough Neagh Sequence**: (7 poems)

    22.3 **3. Bait** – dawdle

    22.5 **5. Lifting** – flail

    22.7 **7. Vision** – fine-combed

24 **Whinlands** – whin

25 **The Plantation** – bleyberries

26 **Shoreline** – currachs

WINTERING OUT (1972): WO

NORTH (1975): NH

1 **Mossbawn: Two Poems in Dedication to Mary Heaney**

    1.1 1. **Sunlight** – pump, griddle, bakeboard, goose's wing, measling, tinsmith, meal-bin

    1.2 2. **The Seed Cutters** – seed potatoes, seed cutters

3 **Belderg** – quernstone, glib, moss, bawn, turf coomb, stubbed

5 **North** – hammered shod of a bay, bleb of the icicle, althing, thick-witted

6 **Viking Dublin: Trial Pieces** – blathering, gombeen-men, pampooties

8 **Bone Dreams** – crock

    8.2 **Bone Dreams ii** – the scop's twang

9 **Come to the Bower** – gorget, glib

10 **Bog Queen** – turf dust

13 **Strange Fruit** – turf clod

14 **Kinship** – spreadfield, bog, bog-cotton, cribs, crannog

    14.2 **Kinship ii** – midden

    14.3 **Kinship iii** – turf-spade

    14.5 **Kinship v** – felloes of the turf-cart wheels, turf mould

21 **Whatever You Say, Say Nothing** – hind tit, drouth

23 **Singing School:** (6 poems)

    23.2 **2. A Constable Calls** – 'spud' of the dynamo

    23.3 **3. Orange Drums, Tyrone 1966** – lambeg

    23.4 **4. Summer 1969** – bog

    23.6 **6. Exposure** – wood-kerne

FIELD WORK (1979): FW

SWEENEY ASTRAY (1983): SA

THE HAW LANTERN (1987): HL

THE CURE AT TROY (1990): CT

SEEING THINGS (1991): ST

THE SPIRIT LEVEL (1996): SL

2   **To a Dutch Potter in Ireland** – slabbery, clabbery, diatomite, ashpits

3   **A Brigid's Girdle** – trindle, handsel

5   **A Sofa in the Forties** – jamb-wall

6   **Keeping Going** – sporran, whitewash, whitewash brush, byre, potstick, tar border, hunkering, buttermilk, hill-fort, reservist, the Diamond, milking parlour, matter

7   **Two Lorries** – cribs

12 **An Invocation** – thrawn, blathering

13 **Mycanae Lookout**

    13.3 **3. His Dawn Vision** – scrim

    13.4 **4. The Nights** – herm

16 **Whitby-sur-Moyola** – bogging in

18 **The Butter Print** – butter-print, awn

20 **'Poet's Chair'** – splay-foot, lea, thorn tree/fairy thorn

21 **The Swing** – plout, townlands, neb

23 **Two Stick Drawings** – drover's cane, blackthorn, briars

25 **The Errand** – stood my ground

26 **A Dog Was Crying Tonight in Wicklow** – corpse house

29 **The Sharping Stone** – sharping stone

32 **At the Wellhead** – midge-veiled

34 **Tollund** – bog-fir grags

BEOWULF (1999): BF

Introduction (page xxiv) – lachtar, scop

Line number		Line number	
5	harrowed	975	hasped
7	reaver	975	hirpling
10	cub	980	blather
11	tholed	1119	sang keens
76	wallstead	1126	forts
82	torques	1174	boons
95	hoked	1352	beyond the pale
140	bothies	1359	keshes
194	thane	2018-9	hand out a torque
287	gumption	2172	gorget
324	war-graith	2212	stone-roofed barrow
419	boltered	2303	gloaming
523	bawn	2321	swinged the land
596	a mizzle of his blood	2433	wean
688-9	bolster under his head	2661	the dangerous reek
707	his shadow-bourne	2774	howe
736	canny	2820	steadfast
787	keening	2903	bane
817	bone-lappings	2909	a wake
848	wound-slurry		

ELECTRIC LIGHT (2001): EL

THE BURIAL AT THEBES (2004): BT

Page numbers, Faber & Faber edition

DISTRICT AND CIRCLE (2006): DC

THE TESTAMENT OF CRESSEID & SEVEN FABLES (2009) FABER & FABER EDITION: TF

Page numbers, Faber & Faber edition

HUMAN CHAIN (2010): HC

AENEID BOOK VI (2016): AB

Line numbers

472 burled

755 scringe